ONCE UPON A GRIFT

FAIRYTALES REIMAGINED FOR LATE-STAGE CAPITALISM

DEXTER DROLL

PETTYFEATHER
PUBLISHING

CONTENTS

INTRODUCTION

Once upon a time, fairy tales warned us about wolves in the woods, greedy giants, and vain emperors. Today, the forests have WiFi, the giants run hedge funds, and the emperors tweet from golden towers. Our world is no less magical-just more absurd.

This slim volume gathers the old stories and dresses them in new suits: bespoke for billionaires, tailored for tech titans, and hemmed with the hubris of politicians. Here, you'll find familiar characters with unfamiliar resumes-princesses with PACs, lobbyists in wolf's clothing, and golden geese on quarterly earnings calls.

Satire has always been the sharpest mirror, from Swift's Lilliputians to Orwell's Animal Farm, exposing the follies of kings, councils, and the crowd. In these pages, you'll find not just laughter but the uncomfortable truths that lurk behind the punchlines. The tales may rhyme, but the realities they lampoon are all too real.

So turn the page, suspend your disbelief, and remember: in the kingdom of power, the fairy tales never end-they just get rebranded.

CHAPTER ONE

THE EMPEROR'S NEW SUIT

There once was a man with a palace of gold,
Whose hair was as loud as his ego was bold.
He ruled with a grin and a permanent pout,
And tweeted decree after half-baked shout.

. . .

This emperor bragged of his fashion and flair,
    Of suits finely tailored and billionaire hair.
    "No one looks better," he'd gleefully state,
    "I'm like if Mount Rushmore could go on a date."

He needed new garments — "The best! Make it grand!"
    "Something so classy the peasants will stand!"
    Two slick little weavers then slithered on in,
    With sharp little smiles and shark-thin skin.

"Dear Sire," they said, "we've got just the thread—
    Invisible cloth, but for brilliant heads!"
    "The dumb can't perceive it, the weak won't endure—
    But you, mighty genius, will know it's couture!"

"Tremendous!" he boomed, "That sounds like a hit!"
    He gave them gold bars and a chair to sit.
    They mimed and they measured with pomp and great
drama,
    While pocketing threads meant for Melania.

Ministers came, one by one, to inspect,
    But none dared admit, "I see nothing direct."
    "It's stunning!" they gasped, all feigning delight,
    "A triumph of taste! A win for the right!"

. . .

The emperor posed in his invisible suit,
    His chest puffed out, his smile resolute.
    "It's slimming! It's strong! It's historically fine!"
    (Though he looked like a roast turkey
    stood up in a line.)

He strutted outside with the press in a swarm,
    The pundits all gasping, "What elegant form!"
    Fox sang his praises, CNN stared,
    The emperor preened, completely bare.

But one child cried out, "He's got nothing on!"
    The crowd fell to silence, the spell nearly gone.
    Yet the emperor scoffed, "Fake news! Just a hater!"
    And kept on parading, two cheeks to the crater.

So let this tale echo, from tower to tent:
    The grandest of fools often bathe in dissent.
    And if ever you're sold what your eyes can't embrace,
    Ask: Is it fashion... or just saving face?

CHAPTER TWO

CINDERELLA: PUMPKIN TO IPO IN THREE STEPS OR LESS

I n a penthouse of glass, high above city grime,
   Lived Cindy, a coder with barely a dime.
      Her stepmom, a mogul with Fortune 500 clout,
And two stepsisters, influencers, always out.

. . .

They flaunted their wealth with a digital gleam,
Posting brunches and brands for the algorithm stream.
While Cindy debugged code and fetched every snack,
Her stepsisters live-streamed their latest attack:

"Cindy, your sneakers are tragically plain.
Try Yeezys, or else you'll be canceled again!"
Her stepmom declared, "You'll never go far,
If you can't monetize trauma or lease a new car."

One day, an invite went viral and wide:
A Tech Ball for founders, with VCs inside.
The Prince was a crypto king, flush with new cash,
Seeking a partner with followers and flash.

The stepsisters preened for their TikTok debut,
While Cindy just sighed-her invite was "blue."
But then came a ping from her Fairy God-Bev:
A unicorn startup, still in beta (but dev!).

With a click and a swipe, Cindy's look was transformed:
A dress made of pixels, her sneakers reformed.
An Uber arrived, coded sleek, self-driving,
With surge pricing waived and five stars for thriving.

. . .

At the Ball, the Prince pitched his next NFT,
  While Cindy just laughed at his blockchain decree.
  They danced through the cloud, they riffed on AI,
  But midnight approached-her code would soon die.

She fled down the steps, left her sneaker behind-
  A limited edition, one-of-a-kind.
  The Prince, undeterred, launched a viral campaign:
  "Find me this founder-I'll fund her domain!"

He searched through the city, he filtered and swiped,
  Till Cindy appeared (her code neatly typed).
  They merged their startups, went viral, went public—
  And left all the haters to troll the sub-reddit.

The moral, dear reader, is easy to see:
  In a world run by moguls and VC esprit,
  You can hustle and grind, or just pivot and flee—
  But sometimes the magic is just good IP.

CHAPTER THREE
JACK AND THE BUYOUT BEANSTALK

Once there was Jack, a broke startup bro,
        Who pitched in cafés and burned
            through cash flow.
"We're pre-product, pre-revenue, super lean,"
He said, as his mom sold their last espresso machine.

· · ·

"Take this to market," she begged in despair,
    But Jack met a banker with slicked-back hair.
    "Forget your machine," said the VC with flair,
    "Try these three beans—seed funding's in there."

So Jack took the deal and came back with a grin,
    "These aren't just beans—they're disruption within!"
    His mom nearly fainted; cried, "We need the rent!"
    But Jack planted the pitch deck and off the beans went.

By morning, the sky had been pierced by a vine,
    Tall as a Series A growth chart line.
    So Jack climbed the stalk with ambition and hope,
    Armed with buzzwords and kombucha and scope.

At the top was a castle, enormous and sleek,
    Run by a giant named Jeff (or maybe
    Zuck-Gates-Musk... Eek!).
    The halls echoed deals, the air smelled of wealth,
    And everything ran on surveillance and stealth.

Jack crept inside and found treasure galore—
    NFT eggs and IPOs by the score.
    A goose in the corner laid golden returns,
    Each one a dividend, fat and unearned.

But then came the GIANT with thunderous pace,

Sniffing out disruption in his venture space.
"Fee-fi-fo-fair, I smell dilution in my share!"
"Is that a founder?" he roared. "Is he pre-cleared?"

Jack grabbed the goose, slid down the vine,
    While swiping a tablet with growth metrics fine.
    The giant gave chase, but tripped on his debt—
    His castle foreclosed by a rival hedge bet.

Back on the ground, Jack launched an app,
    With the goose as his logo and AI for the stack.
    He scaled overnight, got a billion in seed,
    Then sold to SoftBank in record speed.

Now Jack gives TED Talks and wears faux distress,
    "You just need a vision—and way too much press."
    His goose lays coins, but now charges per egg—
    And premium yolks come with terms and a peg.

The moral is clear, if you squint past the spin:
    In capitalism's castle, the thief always wins.
    And if someone offers you a magic bean—
    Take it; just make sure the branding's clean.

CHAPTER FOUR

PUSS IN BOOTS: THE POLITICAL CONSULTANT

T here once was a cat with a taste for fine suits,
　　Who dreamed of a future in
　　high-priced pursuits.
His owner was broke, with no prospects in sight,

But Puss had a plan to set everything right.

He donned his best loafers, his tie neatly pressed,
    And strolled into town as a lobbyist guest.
    He flattered the mayor, he charmed every aide,
    He promised new donors and votes by the spade.

He whispered in ears at the fanciest ball,
    "Back my young master-he'll answer your call.
    He's tough on the issues, he's savvy and bold,
    He's polling ahead, and his platform is gold!"

With spin and with cunning, with headlines and leaks,
    Puss built his man's brand in mere matter of weeks.
    The polls soared sky-high, the rivals grew pale,
    For none could out-charm such a cat with a tale.

His master was crowned with a landslide, no less,
    While Puss got a title and custom-made dress.
    The moral, dear voter, in politics' game:
    It's not what you stand for, but who spins your name.

CHAPTER FIVE

THE THREE LITTLE LOBBYISTS

Once in a swamp near the capital's glow,
　　Three little lobbyists set out to grow.
　　They'd each been interns for donors and hacks,
Now they dreamed of their names on super PACs.

The first built a house out of talking points fast,
　　Thin as a tweet, but designed to outlast.
　　He filed it with buzzwords, reports, and one chart—

"I've got data," he beamed,
"and a graph that looks smart!"

The second built his from polished hot takes,
Recycled from think tanks and donor-backed flakes.
He hosted fundraisers and dodged every fact—
"I'll pivot," he smirked, "then legally redact."

The third took his time and built out of spin,
With influence thicker than three chins of sin.
He crafted a mansion with wings for both parties,
And stocked every room with dark money
and smarties.

But lo! From the shadows came one Big Bad Bill,
Not a person, but policy creeping uphill.
It promised reform, transparency, votes—
It threatened their donors and shamed their big boats.

To the first house it came with a gust and a groan,
"I'll blow down your nonsense, expose every loan!"
And poof! The house toppled—
his "facts" couldn't stand,
He blamed "cancel culture" and fled on remand.

The second house stood, but not for too long,
Big Bill huffed again with a truth-powered song.

The op-eds all backfired, his influencers bailed,
And his hedge fund retreat got subpoenaed and nailed.

The third little lobbyist welcomed Big Bill with a grin,
"I've seen worse," he said, "now let's let you in."
He offered a drink, made a toast to "debate,"
Then buried the bill in a subcommittee fate.

"You can't fight me with data, or morals, or votes—
I've got filibusters in monogrammed coats.
I speak in revisions, I thrive in disguise,
And the people I serve? Well, they always survive."

So Big Bill was gutted, rebranded, delayed—
Then quietly killed in a sub-sub trade.
The three little lobbyists cheered with delight,
As democracy coughed in the darkening night.

The moral? It's eternal, like offshore accounts—
Where power resides, influence mounts.
And if you build your house out of truth or of care—
Be warned: K Street will still be there.

CHAPTER SIX

LITTLE RED RIDING HOOD: A CAUTIONARY TALE OF CLICKS AND WOLVES

O nce in a suburb of fiber and glass,
Lived Red, whose hoodie
was premium class.
Her mother, a blogger with influencer sway,

Said, "Take this DoorDash to Grandma today.

But don't stray from the sidewalk-just follow the app,
    And don't share your data with strangers who tap."
    Red set off, earbuds in, phone in her grip,
    Live-tweeting her journey with every new tip.

But deep in the feed, behind pop-up and spam,
    A Wolf watched her stories and plotted a scam.
    He DM'd her slyly: "I'm Grandma's new friend!
    I'll boost all your posts and your follower trend."

Red, ever trusting of blue checks and flair,
    Sent over her location and WiFi to share.
    The Wolf, a venture-backed predator bro,
    Took shortcuts through back roads
    that Red didn't know.

He reached Grandma's condo, a high-rise with locks,
    And hacked through the Ring cam
    with phishing and bots.
    He donned a disguise-just a filter, not much,
    And waited for Red with a crypto cold touch.

When Red reached the door, she was greeted with glee:
    "Come in, darling Red, and bring that for me!"
    Red paused at the threshold, her phone gave a beep:

"Suspicious login detected;
your passwords aren't deep."

She peered at "Grandma," whose teeth looked so white,
    "Your veneers are suspicious!
    Your jaw's not quite right!"
    The Wolf lunged for Red,
    but she livestreamed the scene,
    And soon all her followers flooded the screen.

A woodsman from Instacart, wielding a broom,
    Showed up in minutes, and swept through the room.
    He booted the Wolf from the WiFi and flat,
    Reset all the passwords, and changed every chat.

Grandma was rescued, her data restored,
    Red learned to beware every wolf on Discord.
    The moral, dear reader, for those on the grid:
    Not every blue check is who they say they are, kid.

So guard your location, your passwords, your hood.
    And never trust wolves, online or in wood.

CHAPTER SEVEN
SLEEPING BILLIONAIRE

There once was a man with a building so tall,
     It shimmered with gold leaf and ego on call.
     He ruled from his penthouse
with bluster and flair,
Shouting "Fake news!" to the clouds in the air.

He dined on McNuggets, declared them gourmet,

Held rallies for mirrors, then sued them for gray.
He'd conquered the world—or at least thought he had,
With a castle, a channel, and three angry lads.

But time, that rude liberal, crept in his face,
With wrinkles that Botox refused to erase.
"Freeze me!" he cried, "In gold-plated glass—
I'll thaw when I'm young, rich,
and kicking some... mass."

They built him a chamber with logos all over,
And packed it with Diet Coke, wigs, and a rover.
His last words were mumbled,
"I'll tweet from the grave,"
As he slid into sleep like a king in a cave.

Decades went by. The news moved along.
His towers kept crumbling, his rights proven wrong.
His followers fled, or forgot, or evolved,
While AI debates were aggressively solved.

One day a group of confused interns found,
The golden cryopod beneath gilded ground.
"What's this?" one asked, as alerts filled the air—
"Oh my god," said another, "Look, it's that hair."

With a flick and a spark and a "Welcome back, Don,"

The pod hissed to life, and the billionaire yawned.
"I'm back! Where's my limo? My empire? My poll?"
They handed him a Diet Coke and a tofu roll.

"MAGA is over, Melania's gone,"
    "The election still wasn't stolen;
    We all know you're a con."
    "Your towers were bought by an AI called Betty—
    Who sold them to liberals to smash with machetes."

He raged and he yelled, "This must be a trap!"
    "You all miss me badly—I'm still king of the app!"
    But no one replied. The interns just streamed,
    "CryoBoomer.exe thinks he's still memed."

Old man tried to pivot, to rebrand, to spin,
    He started a podcast called "Greatness Within."
    But the world had moved on, like empires before,
    And now he was just noise near a vegan food court.

The moral is simple, if morals you seek:
    You can't sleep through change and pretend
    you're unique.
    The past may be golden, but time paints it pale—
    And even Billionaires eventually fail.

CHAPTER EIGHT

THE GOOSE THAT LAID THE GOLDEN EGGS: SQUEEZED FOR PROFIT, PLUCKED FOR PARTS

Once in a boardroom of marble and glass,
Sat moguls and bankers, all greedy for cash.
They owned a fine goose,
with feathers so sleek,

Who laid golden eggs—one every week.

The shareholders gathered, their eyes all agleam:
    "If one egg is good, imagine the stream!
    Let's squeeze her for more, why wait for the rest?
    We'll optimize profits and be the best-dressed!"

They hired consultants, they built a new app,
    They promised returns with a five-minute nap.
    They poked and they prodded, they ran endless tests,
    They gave her injections and wellness-focused vests.

But the goose grew exhausted, her feathers fell out,
    The eggs turned to lead as she waddled about.
    The moguls grew angry, the bankers withdrew,
    The board blamed the workers and threatened to sue.

At last, when the goose gave her final, weak squawk,
    They fired the staff and foreclosed the whole block.
    The lesson, dear reader, for markets and men:
    If you kill your own goose, it won't lay again.

CHAPTER NINE

THE PRINCESS AND THE PEA: ONE PERCENT PROBLEMS

There once was a princess with taste so refined,
She lived in a palace of status and shine.
Her mattresses numbered at least
twenty-three,

Each one imported, hypoallergenic, and free.

One stormy night, she arrived at the gate,
    Demanding a suite and a gluten-free plate.
    The butlers all scrambled, the staff ran amok,
    For pleasing a princess takes millions in luck.

They stacked up her beds in a gilded display,
    But slipped 'neath the bottom a pea out of play.
    She tossed and she turned, she moaned and she wept,
    "My back is in ruins! I barely have slept!"

"Such suffering!" cried her advisors and friends,
    "Let's double the thread count and triple the spends!"
    They tweeted her hardship, the tabloids went wild,
    "How fragile! How noble! How sensitive child!"

The prince was impressed by her pain and her pout,
    For only true royals can whimper and shout
    At discomfort so tiny, so minor, so small—
    A single green pea could unravel it all.

They married in splendor, with caviar tea,
    And built a new wing for her allergies.
    So if you seek status, just whine and decree:
    The world must adjust for your one little pea.

CHAPTER TEN

RAPUNZEL: THE SENATOR IN THE TOWER

In a marble-clad tower on Capitol Hill,
   Senator Rapunzel sat, drafting each bill.
      Her hair, long and golden, a symbol of might,
Was tangled in lobbyists, day and then night.

. . .

Her mother, the Chairwoman, locked her away:
    "Stay safe from the voters, don't mix with the fray!
    The public is messy, their questions too tough—
    Just send out some statements,
    that should be enough."

So Rapunzel legislated, cut off from the street,
    Her donors and PACs sending gifts at her feet.
    But down in the city, the people grew sore:
    "Why's our rep locked up behind marble and door?"

One day, a young mayor, reformist and keen,
    Scaled the bureaucracy, slipped past the machine.
    He called, "Let down your earmarks,
    your red tape, your spin!
    Let's govern for people, not just for your kin!"

They plotted reforms, a bold, public crusade,
    But the Chairwoman thundered,
    "No change will be made!"
    Yet Rapunzel, emboldened, cut ties with her past,
    Let down her gold hair, and joined voters at last.

Now she walks in the sunlight, her tower left bare,
    Remembering power means being out there.

CHAPTER ELEVEN

GOLDILOCKS AND THE BILLIONAIRE

O nce in a tower both golden and tall,
Lived a billionaire king
with no empathy at all.

He'd hoarded three chairs, three soups, and three beds,
Though he only had one body, and two talking heads.

The first chair was huge, all leather and chrome,
It tweeted insults when he sat down at home.
The second was stiff, like a throne made of spite—
He called it "Executive," and claimed it was right.

The last was just perfect: soft, smug, and wide,
Like a podcasting cushion for ego and pride.
He ate three soups daily, with varying flair:
One was too hot, one cold, one garnished with air.

Then came young Goldilocks, broke and fatigued,
Whose rent just went up,
and whose landlord was league'd
With the very same tycoon whose castle stood grand—
Built from tax breaks, grift, and beachfront land.

She wandered inside when the door clicked ajar,
(Security had left to buy Bitcoin in a bar).
She sat in his chairs. One scoffed, one screeched—
But one had lumbar support that truly peaked.

She sipped at his soups. One scorched her lips,
One tasted like stock options and melted chips.
But the third? It was perfect: bone brothy and filling—

Like a TED Talk on bootstraps or tax-free billing.

At last she tried beds, all stacked with faux fur,
    One snored by itself. One whispered, "Yes, sir."
    But one was so comfy, so neutral, so beige,
    She fell into dreams of wealth
    trickling down to her wage.

Then came the tycoon, in loafers of gold,
    Shouting at interns and bragging how bold.
    "Someone's touched my recliner!"
    he gasped with disdain,
    "And messed with my soup! Was it Antifa again?"

He climbed to the room and saw curls on his sheet—
    "A trespasser! A socialist! A lazy elite!"
    Goldilocks woke, stretched, and rubbed at her eyes,
    Then calmly replied: "Your comfort is lies."

"You hoard all these things, but use only one.
    You build bigger castles to block out the sun.
    You gobble up homes, drive the poor to the street—
    And call it ambition when no one can eat."

The billionaire blinked, then summoned a drone,
    And tweeted, "Ungrateful! Go get your own throne!"
    But Goldilocks left, head held up high—

While the tycoon indulged in a luxury lie.

So if you should wander where moguls have dined,
    Check under the gloss for what's left behind.
    For some bowls are gilded, some coins just distract—
    But virtue, dear reader, prefers a plain fact.

CHAPTER TWELVE

SNOW WHITE, SEVEN SHORT-TERM CONTRACTORS AND A POISONED PINT

O nce in a kingdom of hashtags and screens,
The Queen ruled her followers,
Face flawless, so clean.

. . .

Her mirror was smart—an app with a face,
  It measured her beauty, her likes, and her place.
  Each morning she asked it, "Who's trending today?
  Who's got the most clout in this digital fray?"

For years it replied, "You're the fairest, no doubt—
  Your selfies, your filters, your viral callout."
  But one day the mirror, with data refreshed,
  Said, "Snow White's gone viral—
  her posts are enmeshed.

With kindness and candor, no sponcon or bots.
  She's beating your metrics, she's drawing the lots."
  The Queen, in a panic, called up her PA:
  "Find Snow and delete her-she's stealing my sway!"

She hired a huntsman, a fixer-for-hire,
  To shadow and cancel this up-and-comer's fire.
  But the huntsman, on seeing Snow's genuine style,
  Couldn't quite ghost her-he spared her with guile.

Snow White went off-grid, to a co-op of sorts,
  Where seven small coders built indie reports.
  They welcomed her in, though their startup was lean,
  They split all their profits, they kept their code clean.

Snow cooked and she cleaned, but soon took the lead,

And optimized workflows with agile and speed.
The Queen wasn't finished—
she launched a new scheme:
A poisoned device, disguised as ice cream.

She sent it by drone, with a clickbaiting note:
"Try this new flavor! It's trending! Take note!"
Snow took just one bite, and fell into sleep,
Her followers mourning, her metrics ran deep.

But soon came a prince, with a blue verified tick,
He crowd-sourced a remedy, viral and quick.
Snow woke to applause, her brand now immense,
The Queen's reign was over, she'd lost her influence.

The kingdom rejoiced, for a new queen was crowned,
One who went viral for kindness, not clout.

The moral, dear reader, in this influencer age:
True power's not measured by followers' rage.
You can filter your image, you can buy every trend
But the fairest of all is authentic in the end.

CHAPTER THIRTEEN
HANSEL AND GRETEL: THE GIG ECONOMY TRAP

H ansel and Gretel, two siblings quite spry,
Were left in the woods with a
tearful goodbye.
Their parents had debts from a payday loan app,
And "side hustles" never quite filled in the gap.

. . .

They wandered through suburbs
    of foreclosed McMansions,
    Dodging the fees
    and the "Buy Now" expansions.
    At last, they discovered a house made of sweets,
    With logos of startups and VC retreats.

Inside lived a witch, in athleisure and specs,
    Who promised them "equity," snacks, and free tech.
    She hired them quick for her candy-based brand,
    But paid only "exposure"-no cash in their hand.

She worked them all night on her viral campaigns,
    While eating their cookies and mining their brains.
    But Hansel and Gretel, with cunning and grit,
    Reverse-engineered her influencer kit.

They locked up the witch in a blockchain contract,
    Then sold all her candy as "artifacts."

They crowdfunded freedom, then bought out the land—
    And now run a bakery, unionized and grand.

CHAPTER FOURTEEN

THE UGLY DUCKLING: THE POPULIST

In the shadow of monuments, marble and grand,
A duckling was hatched in a bureaucrat's land.
His feathers were plain, his credentials unclear,
The insiders all sneered, "He doesn't belong here!"

The think tanks and pundits, the old party hacks,
Mocked his plain speeches and grassroots attacks.

He waddled through hearings, ignored by the press,
While the swans in their suits called him
"populist mess."

But the people took notice-their voices grew loud:
    "This duck speaks for us, not just for the crowd!"
    He weathered the scandals, the mud and the leaks,
    And soon found his footing with working-class beaks.

One day, he emerged, not ugly but strong—
    A leader who listened, who righted the wrong.
    The swans had to reckon with voters' new clout:
    Sometimes the outsider's what democracy's about.

CHAPTER FIFTEEN

THE ANT AND THE GRASSHOPPER: WORK HARD, DIE ANYWAY

I n a city of glass where the towers compete,
Lived Ant, who worked eighty-four hours a week.
He hustled and grinded from morning till night,

Stacking up assets, defending his right.

His fridge overflowed, his accounts overflowed,
He bought up the block and he widened the road.
"Work harder!" he shouted at bugs passing by,
"Success is for winners-just give it a try!"

But Grasshopper lounged in the shade of a tree,
He played his old fiddle and lived mostly free.
"Why hoard all that wealth?"
he would laugh and he'd sing,
"There's food on the table, and joy in each spring."

But winter soon came, and the city grew cold,
The Ant locked his gates and sat counting his gold.
The Grasshopper knocked,
"Could you spare me a meal?"
Ant glared through the peephole, "You know the deal."

"You wasted your time, you squandered your chance,
You didn't invest in the market's advance.
Now hustle is king, and the lazy must pay.
No handouts for slackers, just hustle or stray."

But Ant found his riches brought little delight,
His mansion was silent, his world locked up tight.

While Grasshopper's laughter still echoed outside,
Among friends round a fire, with nothing to hide.

The moral, dear reader, in towers or glen:
Wealth hoarded alone is worth less than a friend.

AFTERWORD

And so our tales wind down, but the parade of power marches on. The castles may be glass, the dragons may be drones, but the hunger for gold and glory is timeless. If these stories have made you laugh, wince, or wonder, then they've done their work.

Satire, at its best, doesn't just poke fun-it pricks the conscience._Fairy tales once taught us to beware of strangers and question authority; today, they remind us to read the fine print and follow the money. The wolves are still hungry, the emperors still naked, and the golden eggs still tempt us all.

May these fables linger in your mind the next time you see a giant on the news or a princess in the polls. After all, in the real world, the moral of the story is still up for grabs.

The end-until the next chapter.

ABOUT THE AUTHOR

Dexter Droll is a cultural satirist, amateur lexicographer, and full-time observer of modern absurdity. When not revising fairytales for corrupt kingdoms or updating outdated dictionaries for the deeply doomed, Droll enjoys strong tea, weak institutions, and the occasional quiet laugh at humanity's expense.

Hi from Dexter!

I hope you enjoyed my book! If you did, please drop a review on Amazon. It really helps get the word out! QR code below to head right there!

Thanks,
Dexter

🎁 SECRET BONUS!

The Emperor's New Suit

As a special thank you, we've recorded **dramatic audio readings** of three of the most biting tales in this book, performed in over-the-top story-time style!

Scan the QR code above to unlock your bonus and join the secret scroll of email subscribers. We'll send occasional updates & exclusive content.

🖋 SUBMIT YOUR IDEAS!

Have a tale you'd like Dexter to reimagine?

Share your favorite fable, nursery rhyme, myth, or corporate origin story—and it just might get the *Once Upon a Grift* treatment.

Drop your suggestion when you sign up for Dexter's mailing list at the QR code above, or send a raven to hello@pettyfeatherpublishing.com.

www.ingramcontent.com/pod-product-compliance
Lightning Source LLC
Chambersburg PA
CBHW072054040426
42447CB00012BB/3113